CALLING TEXAS

CALLING TEXAS

BERT ALMON

Thistledown Press

Canadian Cataloguing in Publication Data

Almon, Bert, 1943-

  Calling Texas

  Poems.
  ISBN 0-920633-78-1

I. Title.

PS8551.L58C4 1990 C811'.54 C90-097146-0
PR9199.3.A55C4 1990

Book design by A.M. Forrie
Cover painting: "Folded Expanse" by Robert Sinclair

Printed and bound in Canada by
Hignell Printing Ltd., Winnipeg

Thistledown Press
668 East Place
Saskatoon, Saskatchewan
S7J 2Z5

Acknowledgements

Many of these poems have appeared in one form or another in *ARC, The Bloomsbury Review, The Blue Fife, Canadian Forum, Chicago Review, Cumberland Poetry Review, Folio, Galley Sail Review, Iowa Review, The MacGuffin, The Malahat Review, The Midwest Quarterly, Minnesota Review, Mississippi Review, New Letters, Northern Light, Other Voices, Outerbridge, Poem, Poetry Canada Review, Poetry Durham, Poetry East, PRISM international, Queen's Quarterly, Rapport, Rocky Mountain Review, Rocky Mountain Review of Language and Literature, Scrivener, Southwest Review, Trestle Creek Review, Waves, Western Living, Western Review, Whetstone, Writer's Quarterly* and in the anthologies *Dancing Visions* (Thistledown Press, 1985), *Anthology of Magazine Verse and American Poetry Yearbook* (Monitor Publishing Co., 1986-87), *Southwest: A Contemporary Anthology* (Red Earth Press, 1977), *Three Mountains Press Anthology of Poetry* (1976), *Travois: Contemporary Texas Poetry* (Thorp Springs Press). Other poems have appeared in the chapbooks *The Return* (San Marcos Press, 1968), *Taking Possession* (Solo Press, 1976) and *Poems for the Nuclear Family* (San Marcos Press, 1979).

This book has been published with the assistance of The Canada Council and the Saskatchewan Arts Board.

for Olga

CONTENTS

I

CALLING TEXAS

Calling Texas I hear two maternal voices
between the double rings: microwave bleed
gives me faint words in Southern accents.
"Bless his heart, bless his heart." "He just won't
take the breast, I feel like he's starving."
"Bless his heart, don't listen to the doctor,
of course he will. They always do." Me,
I run my tongue over the tiny holes
of the mouthpiece, I'm so oral. I stand
listening between the steady rings of a phone
that nobody answers. The oxygen tank
they wheeled in for my dying neighbour
was tipped with a huge nipple. Listen, baby:
we all take the breast, it's easier than crying
when you know how it works, it's as simple
as breathing, and don't go forgetting that.
Old as he was, my neighbour kept pulling for air.
Somewhere in Texas, an obstinate child
has life shoved in his mouth, and bless his heart,
he wants to push it right out again.
When I'm ready to hang up, I put the receiver
down very softly in its plastic cradle.

Elusive I call you
that manner created
by the high collars
the scarves and bands
you wore over the mark
left by a scalpel
that let in air once
when breathing failed

Elusive like a flashing
of silk, the hypnotic
coin of your affection
shown, then palmed adroitly
till one night I seized
the phantom, carried you
in silence up the stairs
past your parents' room

In bed you took on
substance, and we had
to bite the pillow hard
keeping enchantment quiet
later we woke to find
ourselves wheezing
in a flurry of down

Elusive, you've vanished
like a bright scarf
into the dark sleeve
of indifference, but
I still think of you
gowned in feathers

The young man can't rest his hands anywhere.
The sleepy doctor flaps the dark film
holding it up to the light and laughs,
saying to the girl with the punk cut,
"He's broken both of them. You'd better tell him."
But he's guessed: *"Tous les deux?" "Oui,
tous les deux,"* she answers, and giggles.
"I guess he won't be driving the Cat for a long time."
The fight was over her and he broke his hands
on the other guy and still lost. Somehow
he kept the girl, but her insouciance puzzles him,
and he says *"Tous les deux?"* again, hoping to hear
they're only joking. The doctor is telling her
how these breaks are hard to set, the small bones
don't stay put. He'll instruct the technician himself.
The girl casually lights the first cigarette
that she'll place in her lover's mouth.

You have a gift for leaving me abashed.
One day as we curled up on your sofa,
not quite lovers, you said we were as happy
as two neutered cats. How could I take that
except as a challenge? On a better day,
you lay stroking my skin and asked me
had I heard the old Missouri saying,
"I'd know that hide in the tannery."
Now, my abashment over, I want to tell you
what a fine mole you have on your back.
My hide, your hide, one draped over the other.

You woke me up this morning
and brought in the coffee
We sat up in bed listening
to Sunday FM radio
and the disc jockey's odd tastes:
Beer Barrel Polka performed
by a German choir of 1500 voices
Songs of Fighting Poland
by the Polish Radio Orchestra
and Carrickfergus on a dreamy harp
played by Yeats's granddaughter
When I finished my cup
I could almost hum a blues song
I'm going to write someday
slow but not lugubrious
I'll call it Stirrin' My Baby's Coffee

Albert has left San Remo
(classical music and Italian prints)
for the kitsch of the Canterbury Inn
with its plastic armor and gas logs
blazing in the fireplace
He wanted the bigger tips
                              Or perhaps
he was looking for the right century
Albert was the perfect servant
discreet and unobtrusive
I began to think he'd trained for it
and taken Albert as a stage name
He had only one starring moment
Seeing you he dropped to his knees
and said, "If I profane
with my unworthiest hand
this holiest shrine—"
and you replied, "Good pilgrim
you do wrong your hand too much"
And so I value Albert
Look how skillfully
he has seated you in this poem
and lit the candles of romance
If I falter he'll be back
to pour a little wine
in this pilgrim's glass

As we began the climb into the mountains
we discovered that the Belgian chocolates
had started to melt in the heat
so we had to finish them all—
truffles of ganache and mokka
made into half-moons and hearts
hexads, leaves and medallions—
a delightful necessity
Circumstances always make us
move swiftly from joy to joy

Coming down from the mountains
along the broken stripe of the highway
we saw splendors in every quadrant:
Southeast, the moon rise, northeast
the aurora borealis pulsing
Northwest the remnants of sunset
Southwest the ascent of Venus
Celestial witnesses of our contract
and every time we passed a car
we signed ourselves on the dotted line

Job is a hard one for her:
"I don't want better children,
thank you, and I don't need any camels."
How about a Jaguar, I ask,
the devil rising in me,
putting her to the hardest test.

She's repelled by the revenge
of Jacob's sons on the Schechemites
after the rape of their sister, Dinah.
The sons of Jacob offered a treaty:
become Jews and we will dwell together.
While the Schechemites were still sore
from the circumcision,
the sons of Jacob slew them.
Will this story make it into the feminist Bible?
Con: the rapist fell in love with Dinah
        after attacking her. An improbable change,
        ideologically speaking.
Pro: the sharp justice of the trick,
        poetically speaking.

I ask her what she thinks
of the God of the Old Testament:
"A harsh and irrational old man,
I can't take him at all."
I was asking about God-Our-Father,
not God-your-father, I remind her.

Panelist A, of the feminine gender,
said, "Freud was unfortunately right,
women do feel penis envy, but then,
men feel castrated, so those who don't have it
want it, and those who have it don't really have it."

Panelist B, of the masculine gender, said
"Aren't you really admitting that anatomy
is destiny, or is that hitting below the belt?"

Panelist C broke into the carnival: "Sexist!
That metaphor says all power lies in the penis!"
"No, I'm sorry—it's just a term from boxing."
"Exactly! Have you ever seen women box?"

At that I left, went down to the parking lot,
saw the cold and winking stars
of the Big Dipper hanging far above me,
and I'm not fool enough to say what it looked like.

I know the story about the Victorian lady
who was asked what she thought about
while her husband did that horrid thing:
"Generally I try to imagine new ways to trim a hat"

But I want to know a little more: was she
trimming it with decent veils or jaunty feathers
or adding pieces of wooden fruit
—cherries apples and diminutive bananas
Perhaps she decked it with flowers and a woolly bee
or maybe she topped it with a tiny scarlet bird
that sleeps all night with open eye

I just wanted a good bookcase
solid carpentry, flat paint
We wandered through the place
half-way house for the half-minded
my daughters climbing onto every rocking horse
every chair, both of them clambering into
an empty sandbox
                    The clerk
his teeth too wide for his mouth
his mouth too wide for his face
followed us, mumbling anxious noises
as I dragged a child off a table top
I was sure he fumbled for the words
to ask us to go quietly

I was making arrangements for delivery
with the nervous little cashier
who had to get everything right
if it took three tries
Suddenly the clerk appeared
                        putting a pincushion doll
into the arms of my younger daughter
While I was counting my change
he came back again
                    another doll, larger
for the other daughter
                    I wanted to leave
and whispered to the cashier
            "How much are the dolls?"
He flinched and shook his head

The clerk was approaching with something big
as we left in disarray, coats half-on
Why was I bothered
What refuge do I need
this spasmodic distress
                    in the face of love's small gestures?

If another inch of rain falls this afternoon
we'll go out and help Ivan cover the silage pit

While we wait for more clouds
the little boy watches Aunt Sue knit
and says he's always wanted to try
She gives him a needle and yarn
and he learns to loop and cast-on

Ivan is restless and wants rain
but I've never covered a silage pit
When Meli unpacks her viola
he takes down his electric guitar
and works at the knobs of the amplifier
trying to bring his volume down
without picking up static

The amp should warm for a long time
just as silage needs to soak

Ivan has a clean sound now
and his niece must play up to it
as he tries Old Joe Clark
booming in the living room
a tune for a different kind of fiddle
"It's really part of a scale"
Meli says in her classical way
Do-re-mi-fa-so-fa-mi
                              over and over again
Then Ivan picks out Mansion on the Hill in C
the only key Hank Williams ever knew

Now they play a perfect Faded Love
as the sun comes out for good
Her little brother's yarn is ready to cast-off

I am sitting on the sofa
trying to loop this afternoon
on the needle of my attention

At four years old, a few days after
seeing the movie about Helen Keller,
you were left in the dark
by a power failure, in the tub.
You were sure you'd gone blind. You screamed
for your mother, and when she didn't answer,
you knew you'd gone deaf too,
even with the scream echoing off the walls.
Then she came with a candle
that flickered softly, the way the water
lapped at your hands, spelling its name
the only way it could.

I want to lie here with my eyes shut
Downstairs the notes
one or two repeated
and the occasional run of an octave

The piano tuner started work early

Outside the bedroom window
a robin is singing
Each tone is a squeak
from a child's rubber toy
The bee bouncing against the screen
has the hum of a tiny motor
and tells me it's time to shave

Downstairs the note is middle C
If I keep my eyes shut
I'm the conductor of everything
even the back-up beeper
of a truck in the alley

The piano falls silent
but the clock by the bed—
a small percussion instrument—
has the whole day wound on its spring

Stones purify running water
so then, you're my bed of stones

The Gulf Stream moves temperate
in the chilly stream, so then

you're my warm element
Dolphins rise in their sleep

to breathe, so then you're air
that I rise toward, dreaming

new terms to fit our metaphor

The plane out of Salt Lake City
was full of young Mormon men
in suits with plastic name plates
  Elder Robert Jones
  Elder Wendell Baxter
Nineteen years old, all of them
trim and impeccable missionaries
to the pagans of Baptist Houston

I got all the California champagne
while they drained the bar cart
of apple and orange juice
I began to feel like an oddity
of the local option laws
—the only wet district in a dry county
but I was growing younger by the glass
  Youth Bert Almon, age 41
enjoying God's own fermentation process
(Patented 3 billion years B.C.)
as I watched the procession of bubbles
climbing the glass toward Zion

The first museum we found was the wrong one,
a zoo of stuffed animals, predator and prey
lying down together for once. On the outskirts
we discovered the Museum of the Plains Indian,
low brick as distinctive as school or hospital.

Inside we saw the buckskins and headdresses
of chiefs neatly fitted on faceless dummies.
"Are they stuffed too?" a child asked. Nothing
so cruel. There were glass beads behind glass,
a picture of a buffalo hunt painted on buffalo hide,

and the amulet, a circle of smooth brown stone
figuring the sun, bearing an etched crescent
for the moon, bride of light, and a single point
as the morning star, their child. A warrior's magic,
with no curator's sign to explain his defeat.

The stone didn't burn through the glass, I didn't
carry it off in my white soul as borrowed power.
We just walked out under the big sky of Montana,
where I will never watch the moon and morning star
cross the face of the sun we see by and never see.

for Ernest Tedlock

The collie poked his long nose
into every bush and scrub oak
along the arroyo. My friend,
almost seventy, takes this walk
every day, but it left me panting
on each convenient boulder.
Five ravens coasted on the wind.
Ted pointed out the landmarks
like the Ortiz Mountains.
The organic gardeners hereabouts
buy ladybugs by the gallon
and they all disappear. A hiker
claimed to have seen a meadow
full of them up in the peaks,
a small local myth. It's a dry country:
once on our walk I heard a stream
flowing and turned the trail
to find it was a cottonwood
being shaken by the wind. Even
the sound of water was welcome.
When we climbed to level ground
the collie made for a windmill
and jumped into the water tank.
Afterward, my friend warned,
"When a collie starts to shake,
stand back" He was right.

The dog kept looping off from us,
sniffing his way, but knowing
to avoid the spiny plants.
Near the ranch house was the spot
where my friend wants to build
a small chapel with his own hands.
A medieval gesture, like prayer,
which is meditation made real
by struggle, if people ask him.

That night I kept waking
to wind tossing the leaves.
A long nose got me up in the morning
and I looked out to see water
sopping the caliche: no wind,
but up in the Ortiz Mountains
snow had dusted the ladybugs.

for Stephen Bell

The angry man has learned peace
from the old teacher,
an acre of garden.

Planting the ancient way,
a handful of manure, a handful of clay,
soft blankets for each sleeping seed.

In the ripened heat of dusk
he sits on the ground, silently
laying track within himself,

filling in the blank spaces of his map,
and sometimes, ear to the rail,
he can feel the sound of something far-off,

coming.

She tells me how happy she is
in her small northern town,
with her flowers and garden,
and the woods nearby.
                                    I look
at the album of house and yard,
the pictures of boat and motor home,
and then I see the pages of cartoons
she's clipped out over the years,
all on the desert island situation:
rescue and hopelessness,
the problems of sex and no sex.
She has always sent jars
and bottles into the world,
pickles and relish, the jams
under a plug of paraffin.
I've tasted the wild raspberry,
sweet with a little edge,
the tart flavour of seclusion.

—You're from Texas, know any cowboys?

I don't count the Air Force brat
who rides in rodeos and has a Ph.D.
in something called Instructional Technology
All I know about boots is
they should slip at the heels
and fit snug at the toes
a bit of wisdom I learned
from a clerk in El Paso

But once in Wyoming the station wagon
blew a tire and we wobbled along
to the side road, somebody's gate
where I started unloading all our goods
to get at the spare and jack

A pick-up full of cowboys drove up
facing the gate we had blocked
They changed the tire and reloaded the back
all so quietly they didn't wake the baby

I think that would count

The oils have long since dried upon the canvas,
but the philosopher's chain has the glitter
of genuine gold, and the same colour shines
from the deep folds of his sleeves. You'd think
there was a source of light in the picture, yet
the image can fade a little from the flash of cameras.
Aristotle's hand rests on the poet's head, the bust
that turns up in other paintings as Rembrandt's symbol
of a classic past into which he recedes.
Olga comes here to ponder the painter's
image of the thinker pondering the blind minstrel:
a net of brush strokes holds the human arts.
There's no woman in the painting, but I'm an easel
on two legs and place her in this tableau
of serial contemplation. She is searching
not for the vanishing point but the source
that anoints painted links with pristine light.

glacial valley, Battle River

Just before the farm gate we saw a red fox
running a furrow in a swathed field
far north of his usual range
A second later a red-tailed hawk
swooped low over the highway ahead of us

We came to collect rocks for friends in the city
who have Japanese gardens in their backyards
naturalness elegantly composed

The glacier was not so mannerly
It dribbled stones from its pockets turning back north

At the farm we rode the pickup through the canted fields
Everything is tilted toward the valley bottom
After a while the landscape seemed in motion
We drove past a huge pile of depreciation
(the graveyard of rusting machinery)
to a great mound of stones and boulders
glacial-till lugged here from the fields year after year
From the top I could see two tipi-rings left intact
passed over by the long rakes of the stone-picker

Dizzy on the tilting land
I was brought into an immediacy of stones:
boulders of pre-Cambrian rock   shales and composites
Some striated or polished   some cut into facets
Down at the spring bits of petrified wood
drift to the surface now and then
The landscape still isn't finished
and the spring changes its site   year by year

My son brought me the bones of a cow
delicate veterbrae and ribs
hollow precipitates of calcium
with a little red clinging here and there
We picked samples of rocks with lichens

red and yellow smears on bleak surfaces
(algae and fungi proving-up homesteads)
and filled the pickup with glacial debris
that we would carry back a little way
along the route it came by

At dusk we headed back for the city
with its tiny rock gardens
No sign of the fox or the hawk
agile life on frameworks of minerals
We could see a faint fringe of red on the horizon

I found a leaf in the bed,
brought in with the morning paper.
A little item for the unclassifieds,
I thought. One real object
is worth a thousand pictures.

The woman in the athletics office
said I'd carried in a butterfly
on my shirt. Sure enough,
it clung there in black and white.
It's my badge, I said,
I'm the inspector of fresh air
come to open the windows.

The butterfly headed for the window,
the microprocessor in its head
steering for the nearest light source.
I think the windows are sealed, sir,
that's what the woman told me,
with a poplar tree shaking its pages
through the glass just behind her head.

II

CALLING TEXAS

for Richard Bosley

My friend who studies Aristotle's ethics
had volunteered for a crisis line
he is somewhat misqualified

Aristotle's doctrine of the mean
is like a bright light for candling eggs
but the crisis center is never judgmental
It would teach Socrates the Theory of Valium

Aristotle's rule of excess and deficiency
offered banks for the river of conduct
(If rashness is one bank
and cowardice the other
the brave man sails down the middle)
The crisis center has its own guidelines
Never hang up: even the crank caller
by definition needs assistance

Two thousand years downstream from the Greeks
we don't even see the shores
as our little boats yaw in the estuary

Howard can't explain his research to me—
the flow of energy in living systems—
without mathematics, but he tells me
to think of water seeking its own level.
I visit him after he ruptures a disc
carrying an automobile engine
from the pickup to his garage.
He is considering the papaya juice treatment
(meat tenderizer in the spinal canal)
but there's a death rate of five percent.
"I've calculated my remaining years of life,
statistically speaking, and amortized the risk:
if I have the treatment, I've lost 1.5 years
whether it works or not. It's an acceptable risk."
"No, Howard," I say, "either you live or you die."
"Well, think of it this way. If there were twenty of me,
one would die, but the other nineteen would be cured."
"Howard always objectifies his feelings,"
his wife puts in. I leave him brooding
on alternative statistical models:
his mind constantly seeks its own level
even if it has to flow uphill.

1

Dr. Locke is leaving town
His graduate students are moving him
One is sealing boxes with tape
Another is detaching the cat from the trellis
Dr. Locke has an endowed chair waiting on the coast

2

Dr. Locke is a metaphysician
His favourite teaching story is the blue boat
(better than Russell's patch of red)
Someone replaces parts of a boat for ten years
Someone else retrieves the old pieces
and reassembles them down the beach
Now, which boat is the real one?

Sometimes he spends a week on this story
and never quite launches the boats

3

The graduate students are moving the freezer
while upstairs Dr. Locke is pairing his socks
He wonders if he should match up
similar colors more than similar shapes

Just what constitutes a genuine pair?
Just what makes a theory hold water?

4

The graduate students have put the cat in a cage
Hegel's face stares up from an open box on the porch
and a little rain moistens his eyes

I see Dr. Locke in a blue boat
sailing away over the roof of the garage
to an easy chair on the coast

1

Testimony of The Star Weekly:

ALIEN IMPREGNATES 84 YEAR OLD WOMAN
Doctors Expect Monster Baby in Two Years

I WAS BIGFOOT'S LOVE SLAVE
Trail of Bobby Pins Leads Searchers to Mountain Cave

CURE FOR CANCER IN YOUR KITCHEN
Spice Used Every Day Brings Miracle Results

ANGELS HELPED ME DO HEART SURGERY
Shining Human Figures Hover Above Operating Table

2

The Virgin Mary in North America—
Testimony of Mrs. Veronica Lueker
of Long Island, New York, mother of five:

Our Lady appeared in a beautiful blue mantle
over a robe of purest white.
Her sandals were golden, with fasteners
of precious stones.
                    Next to her stood
Her Son, dressed in a white robe
with a chasuble of rich burgundy.

She alone spoke, saying My child
you must warn the people of the United States
to pray for the Holy Father.
He must throw off his evil counselors,
his life is in danger once again.

Pray that he will be guided to end the wrongs
that have spread through the Church. Bring back
the Latin Mass. My child, warn the people that a fiery comet
will come as a chastisement of iniquity
and three fourths of the planet will perish.
Tell them that AIDS is the first plague from God.

Jesus moved closer and I could see very clearly
the lovely designs in gold worked into his chasuble—

3

Testimony of Sammy Wiggs, petroleum engineer:

At 1600 hours the rain had stopped and an arc of rainbow
formed in the southern sky. Very sharp definition of colours.
To the east of it, another rainbow was hazily defined, more a
smudge of colour than an arc. Between the rainbows I saw what
appeared to be an aircraft descending with its landing lights on.
I surmised that it had flown through the thunderstorm. For a
moment I thought that this plane, bright as it was, could be
taken for a UFO. Then I realized that it was indeed a UFO. It
was shaped like an enormous satellite dish standing on end. It
descended very quickly and quietly, with a rushing sound as it
passed over my house at about 200 meters. When I ran to the
window on the north side of the house, it had disappeared.
There were no measurable effects on the clocks and electronic
equipment in the house. The film in the cameras was unaf-
fected. The vegetables in the garden are growing rather quickly,
but in all regards (size, colour, taste, etc.) are normal. I am,
however, saving the seeds and will see what comes up next
year.

To scamble: v.i. To struggle with others for largesse thrown to a crowd.

Carlos Drummond fixes my kitchen fan free
and tells me he's from the Far East
but Scottish, truly Scottish

Carlos wants to climb the pyramid
of Canadian society quickly
so he shows up one evening
ready to sell me an Amway distributorship
But he calls it sharing an idea
instead of selling
"It's not a pyramid scheme," he tells me
"because everybody gets a share:
it's really an inverted pyramid"

I try to explain that his Canadian neighbours
—McRaes and Changs and Joneses—
have boxes and boxes of Amway
stacked in their basements
but he sits there very plaintive
in his polyester suit and bowtie
and tells me it's the first hope
he's had in years
                    "It's a scam, Carlos
a scam," I say, and he goes away sadly

A few days later he calls to complain
that scam isn't in his dictionary
He doesn't think it's fair of me
to make up words that mock his dreams
as he tries to scale the inverted pyramid

I could remind him that *gang warily*
is the motto of the Drummond clan

After the second drink Harvey
asks the boss for the name of his tailor

After the third drink Harvey
tells me his aunt is the Dalai Lama's secretary
Any time Harvey decides to turn Buddhist
he can administer a financial empire

After the fourth drink he asks
the boss's wife how come she never tried modeling

After his sixth drink
he offers to manage his host's investments
"Let me set you up with bond stripping
and capital gains and you won't be drinking
any more of this wine from screw-top bottles!"

After his last drink Harvey
locks himself in the bathroom a long time
I think it's a shame and want him to open up
There's a gastroenterologist at the party
who should see this marvel of science:
an asshole that sucks

The housekeeper, a blonde ex-hippie,
seemed a silent Martha in the kitchen,
working wonders with pans and paring knife.
One tooth was missing in her ready smile.
After the dishes she brought rum and coke
to the living room and sat on the sofa,
a Mary caught up in Jesus, calling out
his name, praying aloud, giving sermons
to anyone who listened: "I've been
on every trip, drugs, living in groups,
living alone, chanting and meditation,
and believe me, Jesus is the ultimate!"
After the third glass, she picked out
the biggest scoffer, the ex-Catholic
ex-con man turned honest mechanic,
and moved toward him on the sofa, skirt
sliding up to her hips, her voice hoarse
in a triple ecstasy of witness,
and a prayerful man, watching, would've said,
"Lord, look to your handmaiden, she drifts
toward something short of ultimate,
and I can hear the ice turn in her drink."

reading in the grass, asphalt-bounded pastoral
green simplicity with buried sprinklers
bombers climbing from a southward field
trail the thunder of a collapsing tunnel

Samson's temple grows into a world
with no wilderness safe for sages
just a park with a shaking roof
of sonic booms that hammer a hard proverb:

bend a bow until it bends no more
and you'll wish you'd stopped before

Photocopied calligraphy
of a Zen master—
I can hardly believe this gift

"Great Heart" in bold strokes
copied on fine rice paper
with a few black specks
from dust on the copyboard
(I think of Hui-neng's poem:
Since nothing exists
where can the dust collect?)

Like original mind
the machine accepts everything
Office memos, Zen mottoes
or somebody mooning the glass

Black forms on white paper
emerge from the void
as everything else does
Greatheartedness in sheer being
and suitable for framing
The ancient masters
would have copied their backsides
and laughed when the disciples
bowed to the copies

No one goes through a commencement
nowadays except to please parents
or friends, and the rented gown lying
black against my bedsheets was a favour
for my father. The hag of angina
rode his chest day and night, and
he wanted to watch his son become
Master of Arts. He wanted to see
the son's office too, a cubicle
in a library basement nicknamed
the catacombs.

          So we went,
driving the car three blocks,
and I let him go down first
to set the pace on the stairs.
We stopped at the middle landing,
then went on, emerging finally
in a hallway lit by the distorted
spectrum of fluorescent light, muted
by sound-baffling materials. We found
my crypt, as I called it on other days,
cramped space for a desk and two chairs,
and we discussed my future for a while.

We went up again, him first, making
another long stop at the midpoint,
his face gray as the ashes of cigarettes
the doctor no longer worried about.
I watched his lips sucking for breath
as if it lay in mist on a mirror
inches from his face, and later I knew
what he saw reflected there.

Hunting frantically for the marriage licence
the morning of the hearing
I hadn't realized you must prove a marriage
in order to dissolve it
The house looked like a drug raid

The halves of couples milling about
like bisected earthworms
as they searched for the right courtroom
(Monday is divorce day)
So many people dressed up and awkward
their first time in this Singles Club

The big box of kleenex on the witness stand
how the court stenographer would lean forward
and start pointing to it
before the witness knew it was needed

My lawyer slipping out of the courtroom
"I have six other cases this afternoon"
I looked at him quaint in gown and cravat
and thought of the story of the little tailor
who killed Seven at a Blow
Seven flies   of course   not seven giants
no matter how the clients see their troubles

Being the only adulterer who was asked
if by adultery I meant sexual intercourse

Talking to a friend
who was divorced the same day
Telling him my ex-wife
got the tortilla press
Him telling me his ex-wife
got both tortilla presses

Flying over this eroded land
I think of the people it wears
down to a wrinkled beauty
Those skulls on display
teeth ground flat by flakes
of pumice from the grindstone
that broke corn into meal

More fitting than the way
men break themselves down
My friend at Los Alamos
poet and physicist, makes
bombs, and dreams of escape
to live like an Indian
in the Sangre de Cristo range

And at White Sands Proving Ground
another friend, poet and physicist
tests bombs on the computer
a holocaust on magnetic tape
more harrowing than explosions
the tidy printout of blast area
and estimated casualties, broken
down into wounded and fatalities
My friend dreams of heading west
and keeps on punching data
We are near the runway
our shadow a black bird
chasing us on the ground
a stand-off as we plunge
to meet our own darkness
The impact is gentle
cushioned by rubber tires

The street a bright scab over deeper wounds—
the Third World begins just over the bridge
where Santa Fe Street becomes Avenida de Juarez
The strip joints departed with the soldiers of Fort Bliss
but the shops and stands and pitchmen are still here:
"Lady, lady, I'll tell you what I'll do
I'll give it to you at what it cost me
At less than cost, then"
                              There are four of us:
Lee and Beth from Shreveport and Knoxville
Olga and me from Canada
                              I've been here before
and I can measure how hardened I am
by watching them watch the silent beggars
the Indian women and their children
Not a word, just a filthy open hand
One little girl has invented a pastime
She tears gum pulled off the sidewalk
into tiny pieces and sticks them in rows of four
along the side of a building
It's the silence that rings in your ears

Lee has bought silver bangles for his daughter
Olga and Beth are mad about rugs
They want wool with vegetable dyes
and subtle designs   the ones the sellers
have to pull from the bottom of the heap
I look at onyx chess sets and stuffed armadillos
and want to buy nothing
                              (In a month I will dream
I'm dragging an onyx suitcase through a dark airport
and the handle comes off just as I reach my gate)
"Listen, let me talk to you so no one can hear
and I'll make you an even better price"
I hear Beth from Tennessee tell one man:
"You don't understand, I'm a plain dealer"

A salesman shows Olga a switchblade
and explains the gut-slashing thrust to her
At another shop a man tries to sell the plain dealer
a beautifully braided leather whip
We've had enough and cross the street to double back
and won't have to pass the little girl again
We can ransom ourselves with quarters at the toll bridge
and drive the rental car back to the hotel
where Olga's diamond is waiting in the safe
Drinking by the pool at sunset, we watch Mt. Franklin
perform its daily stunt, turning from orange
to violet abruptly, skipping the colours in between

This is one Doukhobor house left unburned.
A Hollywood film-maker turned Canadian
had the inside redone in fine panelling
and put in a stained glass window—flowers,
with the afternoon sun lighting them now.
My fellow guest, Marcus, a professor
of scientific method, outlines his trip
to Shanghai, where he let his brain be picked.
His mind is as orderly as a syllabus:
when research bosses asked him how to ask questions
about reality, he could tell them, 1, 2, 3.
My mind isn't orderly, so I drift into thinking
about the Doukhobors, "spirit wrestlers,"
who burned their houses as a protest
against the state, with cues from the Holy Ghost.
Tolstoy wrote letters that won them refuge here.
Marcus, an old Marxist-Leninist, made
his pilgrimage to China a few years too late:
the true revolutionaries were in jail.
"One fellow I met may have been a true Marxist,
he asked the toughest questions." The Holy Ghost
of history spoke German first, then Russian,
then Chinese. Now it's silent. Nostalgia
is merely a bourgeois emotion. Marcus
knows that as he sits in a lavish house
mourning the class struggle. And I know
he's too constructive to burn anything down.
The dialectic that drives the world is a motor
torn loose from its moorings. Marcus and I
register the vibrations as ironies
as we chat under the stained glass bouquet.

III

CALLING TEXAS

The house needed airing, she said,
and off she went to open all the windows.
I heard her rattling through the drawers
in the kitchen: one fell out onto the floor.
It was a bottle of bourbon she was looking for,
a gift from someone, just to make her sleep.
I didn't want to take her back to the nursing home
half-tight—disgraced at ninety-three,
but I helped her find it, under the sink.
She took drinks from a tarnished tablespoon,
one, two three doses: to make her relax.
the pictures got sorted out, but she couldn't help
with all of the names—you'll know these people,
she'd say. I knew her father, my grandfather,
from the picture on the courthouse wall,
but my dad's keepsakes all went up in a tornado
near Deport, Texas, when I was a baby.
She would giggle girlishly, hand me a picture—
you'll know these—then go on through the box.
After a while she confided that she'd been kissed,
once. That's how she thought of it, being well-bred,
as something that had happened to her. Her father,
the Confederate colonel and one-term judge,
wouldn't have smiled if he had ever known,
but she grinned after she fell asleep in her chair.

(Schedule No. 1, Nominal Return of the Living)

These our fathers
coal miners storekeepers farmers
move across the screen from top to bottom
through the light and into the dark

These our mothers
bearing their husbands' names and children
move to the edge and vanish

The switch under my right hand
will bring them back as I choose
    images on film
    of ink on paper
    traces of traces
bring them back or move them forward
in a blurred streak

Annie MacDonald of Antigonish
had brothers and sisters
who died from the milk of a sick cow
There are too many Annie MacDonalds in Nova Scotia
but one of them must have been my great grandmother
who moved to New England to enter service
who died in East Texas where her Scottish burr
mixed oddly with languorous Southern vowels

The Archives are the only time machine
I move over thick carpets in air so humid
no spark leaps when I'm handed a new roll
with its generations wound on a metal spool

Annie MacDonald of Antigonish
a question with too many answers

After a few hours staring at the screen
I look up and the whole room is flickering
I feel for a moment that someone's hand
is unwinding me in the future

Then my eyes steady and I can see
we are all moving into oblivion
at the constant speed of time
with Annie and her brothers and sisters
shadows of shadows

Our fathers and mothers shelved in cabinets
pray for us now and as we disappear

William Bryson, 1866-1920
Maggie Bryson, 1871-1936

1898

Someone must enter the baby's name
on the record page of the family Bible.
She would do it herself
if she could stop crying.
They think she's crazy,
her husband and daughters,
but she knows what to write:
    Mary Dolane Bryson
    April 29, 1898—September 26, 1898
Exactly four months and twenty-seven days.
She would enter it on the parchment page
between the Old and New Testaments
if she could stop crying.

1899

Mr. Bryson, newly come to Redwater,
is too genteel for a lumber trucker,
the landlady thinks. She gathers he kept a store
in a town to the west. Even with three daughters
he's worth thinking about, a widower
with such good manners, serious
through and through, not a trifler.

After a while she gives up:
he never appreciates the special desserts,
the sewing she does for his daughters.
The man isn't serious. In fact, she thinks
a little sadly, he isn't even a trifler.

1910

A strong woman, she runs the ward now,
the nurses give orders through her.
She gets letters from Maudie, a daughter

who doesn't fear the taint of madness,
and some from a man who pretends to be Bill.
People never stop trying to humor the mad.
Bill must be dead: her rings were taken away.
But she's going to be buried with them.
Even a widow has some rights.

1912

Bill Bryson toured the backwoods of Texas
with his fighting bears. Three hundred dollars
in ready money for any man who could outwrestle one.
The bears, muzzled and bipedal, never lost a match.
In Texarkana a fellow with a cud in his jaw
looked at the she-bear and her cub and said,
"That must be his wife and daughter."
Bill laughed along with everyone else,
then coaxed the cracker into the ring
to try his skill with Mrs. Bryson.

1918

The photographer set up the camera
at the doorway, and the light is strong.
Tobacco in the cases at the left,
candy on the right, baskets of fruit
in the middle. Joe, the one-handed clerk,
stands on the left, letting the black glove show.
Centered on the back wall is a poster
for Fatima Cigarettes, the veiled lady.
the store is decked out for Christmas,
streamers along the lath ceiling converge
on a paper bell. The owner is leaning
on the candy counter. Twenty years a widower,
and his daughters are respectably married now.
He has a curio on the counter, the fabled monkeys:
Hear-No-Evil, See-No-Evil, Speak-No-Evil.

the image

This is the only fountain of youth:
the triple bath of toxic chemicals
to develop, stop and fix a print
after the new negative has been retouched
with the spotting brush and etching knife.
The fresh image comes from the last solution
with scratches and water stains wiped away
and the contrast heightened: as good
as new, the photographer says, even
a little better than it was in 1890.
He won't quite say he improves on life.
This is my great-grandmother, one glimpse
of her nature captured in a Texas studio.
With what pains we can be true to the past.
We are the evidence of its fidelity to us.

a caption

I find her beautiful, with a touch of reserve
in the face set over a high, ribboned collar.
She looks away from the lens, to the left.
I would see her as an austere woman
if I hadn't heard the one anecdote:
when the black hired man's wife died
in childbirth, she nursed the baby,
against the opinions of a rebel South,
and was indifferent to how many times
the parents had been bought and sold.

Mary Lora Smith, 1854-1928

The girl came with a suitcase.
"Please help me. I'm your sister,
we had the same father."
                              "Go away,
my father would never—
                    he was a good man."

Shutting the door, what could she do now
but look for sinners in her own husband and son,
never turning the lock for that ghost, half-
sister, half-father?

My father's dog tag lying in a drawer,
the name misspelled, the date correct.
A disc struck off, like me, in wartime,
a time of tending buoys and driving trucks,
of slipping off to sleep in his own bed
with his new wife in a roach-filled room.

I rub the metal of my inheritance,
its letter worn smooth by years on a chain,
years that began before my memories.
Those days shut tight to recollection
will open a little to hearsay and snapshots:

the fragments of a man's life in a drawer
for another tag of his existence
to hold in hand and read correctly.

Waiting for the cake to cool, the mother,
high-strung housewife, told a story:

The gingerbread man leaped from the oven,
lost his eyes and buttons to the birds,
limped a trail of crumbs through the woods,
made two messy mouthfuls for a clever fox.

Waiting for the cake to cool, the boy
thought how much better to wait in the pan,
the buttered pan, for a nervous housewife
to make neat slices with a moistened knife.

My mother was six in 1931, the year
of Karloff's *Frankenstein.* When the monster
and the little girl began to play
by the lake, tossing flowers in the water,
my mother stood right up in the *Strand*
and yelled out, "Run, you crazy fool, run!"
That scene was soon cut from the film.
A few years later, a strange man sat by her
in the dark and ran his hand over her body.
She didn't yell, not knowing what would happen
if she did.

I can't imagine her as a child
when there are no snapshots—a cold family—
so I always visualize a Shirley Temple
in curls and cuteness. More than forty years
after *Frankenstein,* her uncle Eli was coming
for a visit, and she broke out in a rash.
Finally she realized the strange man
hadn't been a stranger. Memory made the cuts
it had to, but the body remembered
the monster wearing a family face.

"Get scared enough," my father said
"hair turns colour overnight, it can"

Six years old, on a Christian errand
"Go play with Molly, home from the Home"

I met her in a backyard, under cedars
sitting on a bench in her outsized clothes

Her eyes blue and unfocused
her hair the colour of cotton

and her skin the colour of indoors
At sixteen unable to speak one word

Just facing my way, back for a week
Molly the heavy cross of her parents

What had scared her, I asked myself
looking into her eyes   She looked back

and I ran home crying, no charity
in me at all, hiding in the bushes

from noon, coming in at suppertime
to climb upon a vanity bench

and look into a tear-filmed mirror
to check the colour of my hair

Those Texaco family picnics:
up to their necks in ice
bottles of bright gaseous
liquid tinged with flavour
as many as I could drink
and never more than seven
before hiccups finished me
I wanted to drink my age
farther behind each picnic
The men drinking the free beer
failed in their own attempts

The bounty of the company:
the island rented for the day
barbecued ribs and baked beans
none of it called soul food
though all the cooks were black
I remember the strange feel
of plastic forks scraping
against dampened paper plates

And the rides were free;
cups'n'saucers, bumper cars
trailing sparks at the wheels
But the roller coaster
was off limits for me
I'd break my neck
or lose that lunch
as the car cracked the whip
of the climbing tracks
I dreamed of being old enough
to decide for myself
and old enough to play
the game favoured by the men
The water tank, a black man
sitting on a plank over it

Beside him a bullseye
in black and white, the object
to throw a ball dead center
The plank fell, and splashing, laughing
the black man would climb out
out and up to his uneasy eminence
I knew good will when I saw it
Someday I'd wear refinery gray
line up with the others after beer
and my roller coaster ride

But now the letter from home
that unsealed all these memories:
"The pleasure peer rollacoaster burned down
they might build it back but nobody goes there
only the colord people nowadays and you know
they are everwhere, like I told you last letter
they broke in and stole the gun collection
and how do they expect us to defend ourselves
without even a gun in the house?"

My small townspeople
I think you can float
a bond issue to rebuild
the roller coaster, but how
will you ever get a black man
to take his place again
jovial over the water tank?

The sun raises sparkles on a concrete porch
where a girl just over the doorstep of puberty
(her nipples like twin buttons under the shirt)
is eating the red heart of a melon slice
down to the green rind, exuberantly spitting
seeds beyond the iron railing into the grass.
Her brown curly hair shakes like heat ripples
as she laughs in flirtation with neighbour boys.

That image sets me down on a wooden porch,
the light stroking a gloss into the gray paint,
where my cousin Linda and I, both eight, sat
in giggling exile as the doctor inside performed
the secret post-partum rituals on my mother.
Our backs were to the door, and through it
my new sister was crying as we sat roasting
our feet and haunches on the splintery wood
and ate tomatoes, the bribe for our absence,
a shaker of salt between us.

                       No one recalls
a taste, but a laughing girl summons back
our furtive chatter about sex and birth
(how babies are conceived by touching tongues)
and I see the red fruit in my hand, the seeds
suspended in time, still floating in fluid cells.

Al, the quiet shoe salesman next door
was a dumpy fellow distinguished only
for a succession of beautiful wives
At least, they were supposed to be wives
but my parents had their doubts

The most beautiful one was Toni
with her long hair and blue eye shadow
the first woman I really noticed
She came over the morning after a concert
holding a signed album by Belafonte
"Isn't he the sexiest thing?" she exclaimed
waving the cover at my East Texas mother
who said later, "I knew they weren't married—
her showing that coloured man's picture
with his shirt unbuttoned down to his navel"

I was puzzled, not understanding
the swashbuckling logic of adults
The way one syllogism sails up
to another and a gang of connotations
swarms over the rail shouting oaths
just like pirates in the Caribbean
in the old days, before calypso

My father's best friend was called Nooky,
even by my mother,
and I grew up thinking this was his name.
One day in my teens it hit me,
but nobody would explain.
Nooky would come for visits with Mrs. Eels,
his stepmother or guardian or aunt or something,
an old lady with triple beads and purple eyelids.
She always brought her chihuahua—
always called honey, and always horny:
it would mount her foot, a chair leg,
the floor lamp, anything,
and hump away, its red member
quivering with prodigious lust.
Mrs. Eels never noticed these activities
of the little dog—an embodied penis—
though when the priapic pooch grappled her leg,
the tea cup would rattle in her saucer.
Nooky and my father would go on reminiscing
about their days in the Coast Guard,
adventures nautical and comic, but never erotic.

Prodded by his parents, the boy walked down
the aisle during the last chorus of the hymn,
shook hands with the trackstar who could run
the mile for Jesus in four minutes flat.
The athlete-evangelist had a plane to catch,
so the gray minister with the weak handshake
took over, led the convert to a changing-room
where white robes fleshed the hangers, and gave
instructions in the ritual, not the faith.

The baptistery was heated for every service.
A mural of Jordan's valley lined its walls,
the curtain drew back for each performance.
The boy went down for the third name, the pad
held to his face by a weak hand turned strong.
Water pounded his ears with a rushing sound
but no tongue of fire touched his shoulder
when he came up in dripping white, face dry,
a shaking ghost, unsanctified forever.

I learned about the evils of dancing
from Brother Coffman, church janitor
and ex-engineer (he was always telling
how he heard the first torpedo go off
and almost, almost stopped the train
before the report of the other fired him).
He took me aside one Sunday after church
and explained it all: "You've been asking
people what's wrong with dancing, well,
maybe nowadays kids don't touch so much,
but back in the days when I started work
for the railroad, we always called it
belly-rubbing, *hey, let's go to the dance hall
and do a little belly-rubbing,* we'd say."
Here he paused, eyes almost shut, relishing
the memory, "so when you start wondering
if you should do it, just keep in mind
what the old engineer said, it's a terrible sin
and temptation, it's nothing but two
hot bellies rubbing together."

Going home from church, my eyes
almost shut in contemplation, I left
the warning far behind me on the track,
my adolescent throttle wide open, hoping
for a bigger explosion down the line.

Lunch hour in the school parking lot, time
for forbidden cigarettes and talk, and Jim's GTO
was the place where he stripped off his shirt
to exhibit the long scratches Louise had left
as she called for *more, more*, in the very back seat
where his friends listened to his bragging.

We envied the fast car and faster woman,
but it never occurred to me to admire
their responses to the driver until the year
Louise was speed queen of my typing class,
and I imagined those red-nailed fingers
tapping out *more, more* in steady strokes.

In the shopping centre the tantalizing goods lie
in a blaze of cold light and wait to be fondled
but at sunset I discover a new attraction
a compound at the edge of the parking lot
RIDES FOR EVERYONE and THE WORLD'S TAMEST ANIMALS
                BRING YOUR CHILD TO FEED THEM

The sun is stroking the mountains as I enter the gate
to meet the thrusting nuzzling mouths of goats
donkeys llamas calves pigs tapirs and more goats
Tickled past laughing I push them away
                                        a tug at my ankle
a goat is chewing my cuff
                        I break loose
He begins to nibble a candy wrapper
blown against the outside of the fence
drawing it through the wide mesh with his tongue
Looking away I see the sun ignite the clouds

A giant tortoise lies in the sawdust too defeated
to retract itself as horned animals nibble at its limbs
A boy beats the shell with his fist
                                sound of a drum
as the sky burns soundlessly
                        A child is screaming
overwhelmed by polymorphous perversity
of crowding, sucking animals—

The wind rises and cracks a whip of sawdust
in my face

At the small merry-go-round the pimply operator
is calling for children   His eyes are bright with liquor
"Last ride of the night   absolutely free   no tickets
last ride   get on   everybody get   on   last ride"
The clouds are cinders when his hoarse voice stops
and the creaking machinery begins

                                    He hops on too
"I left the switch open
                        We can ride all night"

My vision of the bright wheel turning in the dark
is blurred by the lash of sawdust
but I am sure this is a hell for the childish
and the ride will never end

I remember the parlor filled with gutted pianos,
no space to walk freely. Your husband repaired them,
he worked at night, that's why
no one ever saw him. There was a blackboard
covered with pulse and blood pressure readings.
When we shook hands, you left chalk dust on my fingers.
I walked into the humid Texas heat, no breeze off the Gulf.

Now your car has bullet holes
from the days he went target shooting
in the country. He drank.
One night he took four shots at you,
then found a closer target. The Police
held you till they were sure he was left-handed.
Then you could go home, help the neighbours tidy.

What has this small town, with its country stations,
its dozen brands of Baptists,
the splinters of Holiness churches meeting
in rooms over garages, what has it offered you—
the Catholic girl who liked to read and play the piano?
Classes in Oriental mysticism from an eccentric rabbi,
part-time jobs playing honky tonks on Saturday nights,
church organ on Sunday mornings.
You drive that riddled car hustling work.
One front tire is bald,
it could send you into the curb or median anytime.

The hot days are bad for your heart.
When it begins to fibrillate
you take pills and sit quietly in a dark room.
When it's really bad you call my mother and talk,

not wanting to die alone. It races, races,
sometimes it speeds up so much
it seems to be trying to leave you behind.
But you sit still, determined to play out your engagement.

I do an inventory of losses each time I visit
The marker for the child killed by an alligator
terrified me when I was a child
(I wondered if there was anything left to bury)
but now it has been discreetly removed
My parents' ruined house is ruined a little more
Even the red condemned notice is gone
along with the fig tree where I spread my blanket
and read *Uncle Remus* and *Robinson Crusoe*

The spirit messages told Arthur Stilwell
(insurance genius and friend of Conan Doyle)
to build a railroad from Kansas City to the Gulf
and found a great city there
I don't see any signs of greatness
in this southern town with its palms and magnolias
wedged between the canal and the refineries
Now it has been split by the Interstate
(the America of tall signs and exits)
Modules of housing and shopping centers
replace the right and wrong sides of Stilwell's tracks

But simple myths of decline and freeway culture won't do
In the M Bank a Vietnamese teller works with a black trainee
A town that saw everything in black and white
has three blocks of Vietnamese shops and offices
and a thirty foot statue of Mary in a pagoda